D0093280

Youth
Materials
Grant
1999

POPCORN

POEMS BY
JAMES STEVENSON
with illustrations by the author

GREENWILLOW BOOKS, NEW YORK

Copyright © 1998
by James Stevenson
Greenwillow Books, a division of
William Morrow & Company, Inc.,
1350 Avenue of the Americas,
New York, NY 10019.
http://www.williammorrow.com
Printed in Hong Kong by South
China Printing Company (1988) Ltd.
First Edition
10 9 8 7 6 5 4 3 2 1

Library of Congress
Cataloging-in-Publication Data
Stevenson, James, (date)
Popcorn: poems / by James Stevenson.
    p.   cm.
Summary: A collection of short poems
with such titles as "Popcorn,"
"Driftwood," and "My new bird book."
ISBN 0-688-15261-9
1. Children's poetry, American.
[1. American poetry.]   I. Title.
PS3569.T4557P67
1998   811.'54—dc21
97-6320   CIP   AC

For Matthew and Peter

Contents

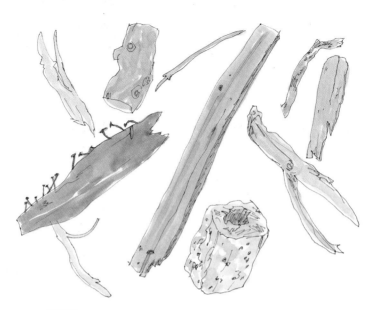

Scattered along the beach today
are logs, branches, tree trunks,
boards, sticks, planks, and railroad ties.

When did they get here?
How far did they come?
How hard was the trip?
How long will they stay?

Some may stay for years and years,
Sinking in the sand.
Others will leave on the first high tide.

But which is which?
When we come back tomorrow,
We'll see.

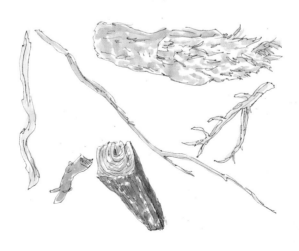

At Henry's farm
They all speak Geese:

"Nk gnk ng kng gn nk?"
"Gn gk gng ng guk."
"Kng gnk gn nk kng!"

The hot dogs, the mustard,

The paper plates, the ketchup,

The napkins, potato chips,

The lemonade,

The chocolate cake and ice cream—

All gone.

But under the apple tree

The table waits

For next time.

Under the hull of the *Dorothy B.*,
Where schools of bluefish swam,
Where dolphins rolled,
A golden dog lies sleeping
In the shade.

SOMETHING'S BROKEN? JUST CALL TOM. HE'LL FIX IT. EVERYTHING HE NEEDS IS IN HIS TRUCK.

SOMEWHERE.

Chelsea dances around me
   as I make her breakfast,
Encouraging me to make it
   bigger, better, more delicious.
Then when I put it on the floor,
She takes a look,
   and steps back stunned.
"Is this for me?
   You call this breakfast?"
She leaves the bowl alone, and goes
   into the other room to brood,
Allowing me ample time
   to improve the dish.

But I will not change her breakfast,
and she will not touch that slop.
I leave, and in a while I hear
a lapping sound.
I look through the door.
She's wolfing it down,
her tail wagging.
It was only a matter of principle.

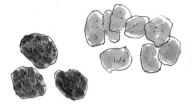

A GOOD THING
ABOUT THE BAKERY IS—

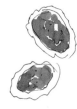

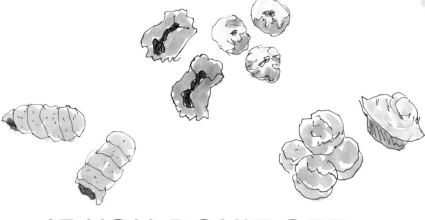

IF YOU DON'T SEE
WHAT YOU WANT,
YOU'LL WANT
WHAT YOU SEE.

You could say this isn't much of a morning:

Cold mist across the meadow,

The woods in tatters,

Fog horns bleating.

The ocean drones like traffic on a highway,

Towels hung out to dry are dripping from the line. . . .

When suddenly

From around the side of the house

A soft wind comes,

Carrying the smell of lilacs.

At midnight in the All-Star Restaurant
They put the chairs on the tables
Upside down.

They swab the floor.
They lock the door.
They all go home.

But some say there are ghosts
In the All-Star Restaurant. . . .
If you were there around 2:00 A.M.,
You might hear ghostly whispers
Coming from upside-down chairs:

"Let's see . . . a BLT for me."
"Maybe I'll try the meat loaf."
"I think I'll have the chef's salad, please."

It was spring, and midnight.

A skunk ran across the road.

He was moving fast,

But in the headlights

I could swear

He was wearing

A tuxedo.

*i*n the morning fog
   You see a boat at anchor—
      Then it's gone.
There's another—
Now that's gone.

Here's a person in a rowboat,
    rowing.
Now, no rowboat—
Only oarlocks creaking
In the fog.

The Mack truck and the shovel
Are neighbors in the weeds.
"You used to lift a lot of dirt and rock
In the old days, didn't you?"
     says the Mack truck to the shovel.

"Tons and tons," says the shovel.
"Didn't you haul heavy loads
 All across the country?"
"Sure did," says the Mack truck.
        "Miles and miles."

 The weeds bend in the breeze.
"Those were the days," says the shovel.
"Darn right," says the Mack truck.

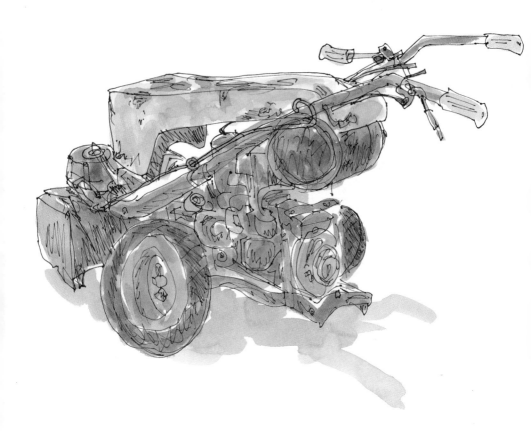

If you knew what to turn,

If you knew what to twist,

If you knew what to push and pull

And snap and click

And crank and yank,

Then this machine would probably do

Whatever it is

It's supposed to do.

Gentle black dog.

She stands stock still

And lets the infant poke her in the eye.

Then she walks away,

Saving herself for later

When the child is old enough

To need

A gentle black dog.

Long gone from the ocean,
Hollow and dry,
What's left of the crab still says:
This was one tough customer.

You don't believe in flying saucers?
Go to Aldo's Pizza.
Flying saucers
Spin in circles
Over Aldo's head.

You don't believe in knights and dragons?
Go to Aldo's Pizza.
See Aldo's gallant nephew Larry
Lance the fiery dragon!

You don't believe in sorcery?
Watch Dominick the sorcerer
With four swift strokes of his magic wand
Turn joy for one to joy for eight!
It's all at Aldo's Pizza.

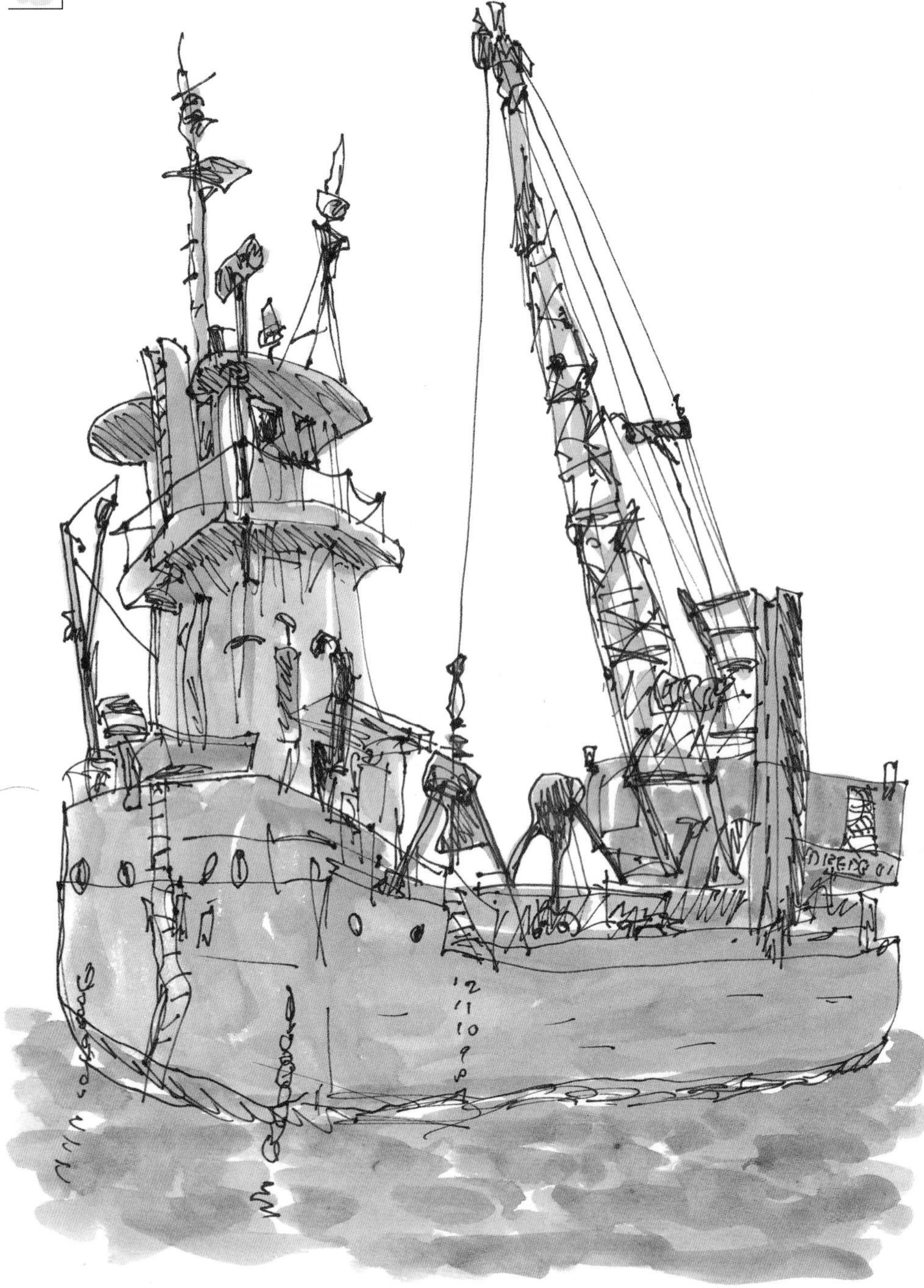

The dredge dredges sludge:
Sludge like fudge,
Sludge that won't budge,
Sludge you wouldn't care to tudge.

Dogs go in the back seat,
   Always in the back seat,
Miles in the back seat,
Hours in the back seat.

But in the parking lots of shopping centers,
You'll see: Dogs get their chance
At last
To drive.

They're hammering in stakes,
They're putting up tents—
Something's happening
On the village Green.
Don't know what it is,
Or when it is.

I'm going.

Out of the fog

Crept a raggedy cat.

You could tell

By the way he moved,

You could tell

By the way he turned,

He was a pirate,

And the fog

Was his ocean.

Suddenly
A wind
Has come up,
Sending
The gray clouds
Flying.
And
Suddenly
It is
Such a beautiful day,
You can hear
The trees
Cheering.

Sitting in the treetop
Was a small bird—gray and pink.
It might have been a sparrow[1]
Or a chimney swift[2], I think,
Or else it was a warbler[3]
Or a jaybird[4] . . . then again,
A nuthatch[5] or a swallow[6].
But I think it was a wren[7].

[1] page 190
[2] page 98
[3] page 76
[4] page 140
[5] page 152
[6] page 137
[7] page 158

At the ice cream place
They've got
Chocolate Raspberry
Mocha Chip
Vanilla Fudge
Orange Pineapple
Strawberry
Black Raspberry
Pistachio
Peach
Butter Crunch
Which would Chelsea like the best?

We can't ask her.

She can't tell us.

She always gets

Vanilla.

Sometimes when you go out at night,
You think there are no stars.
But, in a minute, they deck the sky in all directions.
Some days the radio says snow will come,
But you don't see it
Until the single flake sails past the black tree.
This morning I wished for April,
But it was still March—cranky and bitter,
Ice on the sidewalk, snow in the shadows.
The wind said, Go inside and get yourself a hat.

But when I turned, there among the dead brown leaves
I saw a purple rocket, no bigger than a baby's thumb,
Just arrived from the center of the earth, bearing a message:
<u>*Soon*</u>*.*

White gulls walk around
the baseball field.
The mallard ducks call,
"Get a hit—get a hit!"
At last a single gull takes off
like a hard line drive—

The Canada geese say,
"Hmpf. Hmpf."

Like it or not,
The morning mist
Takes away the ocean,
Removes the sky,
Erases the field and hills,
And like a patient teacher
Starts us again
From the beginning:
The sounds of birds, and a yellow wildflower.

When Walker and I bought our movie tickets
    and went into the lobby,
There were brown boxes
    stacked seven feet high
And ten feet wide
And twenty feet deep.
You could hardly get by.
What was this cardboard castle?
We took a close look.
On every box was printed one word
In small letters:

P O P C O R N

"Could you eat that much popcorn?"
    said Walker.
"I already have," I said.

Out the train window
Backyards are passing,
Heaped with Don't-Need-It,
Where-Else-Should-We-Put-It,
Someday-We'll-Want-It,
Why-Did-We-Buy-It,
Wait-Until-Later,
Forgot-It's-Still-There.
Front yards are boring.
Backyards tell stories.
Out the train window
Watch them pass by.

It's late in December.
A cold wind is blowing—
Why are those people
out there on the mud?

Each has a rake
and a pail or a basket—
Looks like they're dancing—
Dancing for clams.

*D*eep in the woods
There's a busted TV,
Half full of leaves,
Resting against a log.
Maybe it's turned into a watcher by now.
Maybe it sees the local shows:
"Deer Crossing the Narrow Brook,"
"Ferns Bending in the Wind,"
"Snow Floating Down Through the Trees."

Chelsea is gone.

Her water bowl is dry.

Her green collar lies in her empty dish.

The dog door that flapped when she
went in and out is silent.

Beside her bed her teddy bear sits waiting.
In these last days
When we called Chelsea's name,
She hurt too much to come.
But we knew where she was
By the thumping of her tail on the floor.
And we could go to her
And kneel down
And put our arms around her.

On the back porch this morning
Threads of yellow silk
Are scattered where the corn
Was husked at twilight—
Zig-zags, scribbles, loops, and swirls.
I'm not quite sure,
But I think they say,
What a party!